THE QUESTION OF THRACE.

Greeks, Bulgars and Turks.

BY

J. SAXON MILLS, M.A.,

St. John's College, Cambridge; Barrister-at-Law, Inner Temple.

AND

MATTHEW G. CHRUSSACHI, B.A.,

Magdalen College, Oxford.

LONDON;
EDWARD STANFORD, Ltd., 12, 13 & 14, Long Acre, W.C.2

1919.

Foreword.

THE Thracian question is, on the whole, less familiar outside the Balkans than any other of the problems connected with the Peninsula. The present is, so far as we know, the first monograph on the subject which has appeared in this country. As a result of this unfamiliarity with the issues involved, we have the paradox that at least till 1915 European public opinion, especially in England, regarded as inevitable and natural that very solution of the question which, to any one with the facts before him, must appear the least admissible of all, viz., the annexation of Thrace to Bulgaria. The events of the last five years have changed the situation and brought a rival solution to the fore. As early as September, 1915, the Entente Powers offered concessions in Thrace to the Government of King Constantine in return for the entrance of Greece into the war. In February of the present year the Greek claim to three-quarters of Thrace was formally submitted to the Peace Conference in Paris. The peace-treaty of Neuilly (November 27th, 1919), by pushing back the Bulgarian frontier from the Ægean secured an essential condition of the realisation of this claim. Even to-day, however, there is a tendency in certain quarters to regard the Greek claim in Thrace as an "Ersatz," something that could be thrown overboard without much ado in return for concessions elsewhere. Such a view is wholly erroneous. In any consideration of the Thracian question we must not lose sight of the fact that Greece has already sacrificed her historic rights to her ancient capital, along with half a million of her nationals, to the necessity of internationalizing Constantinople and the Straits. Even if the formulated Greek claims are all satisfied, including the claim to Thrace, only 65% of the Greek race will be thus included within the frontiers of the Greek State. Such a moderation has not been shown by any other State which had an "Irredenta" before the War. It should surely strengthen rather than weaken the claim advanced by Greece to Thrace, especially if that claim can stand on its own merits.

Yet the facts that ought to be decisive are easier to establish here than in the case of any other Balkan problem.

In the first place there are in Thrace no amorphous populations, as in Macedonia, alternately claimed as Bulgars, Greeks and Serbs by rival propagandas. In Thrace the lines of cleavage between the various races which compose its population are very clearly marked. Greeks, Turks and Bulgars alike are perfectly race-conscious, and the rare instances in which the frontiers of nationality and language do not coincide are not such as really to complicate the problem. Even the relative strength of the three chief elements of the population can be fixed without much difficulty. The Turkish and Greek statistics available tally with remarkable closeness, if we allow for the considerable interval between the dates of their publication. The Bulgarians have never published a complete set of figures, but copious evidence of other kinds is available from Bulgarian sources. So true is this that the present volume, while involving a refutation of Bulgarian claims, is primarily based on Bulgarian data.

In 1917, Dr. Dimitri Rizoff, then Bulgarian Minister at Berlin, published a volume in four languages, (German, English, French and Russian) on "The Bulgarians in their historical, ethnographical and political frontiers." In view of the wide publicity given to this work and the status of its author, it may fairly be taken as the most authoritative statement that has appeared of the aspirations which Bulgaria sought to realize by entering the War. It consists of a lengthy introduction signed by Dr. Rizoff and outlining "the bases on which a durable peace in the Balkan Peninsula can and must be reared," and also of a large number of *pièces justificatives* in the shape of historical and ethnological maps. The historical maps were specially drawn and annotated for the book by Prof. V. Zlatarski of Sofia University, while the ethnological part of the work was entrusted to Prof. A. Ischircoff of the same University.

The avowed purpose of the book was to assert the Bulgarian claims as against Serbia and Rumania in the Dobrudja, the Morava and Timok valleys and Macedonia. Only a passing and somewhat cryptic allusion is made in the Introduction to Greece which had only declared war a few months earlier. Incidentally, however, the book affords very substantial evidence, and evidence the more valuable as it proceeds from a Bulgarian source, in refutation of any Bulgarian claim to Thrace. The fact that at the time of the publication of this work Thrace was still partitioned between Bulgaria and her ally Turkey does not make it any the less significant that Zlatarski's maps prove Bulgaria to have no historical right to Thrace, and that the ethnological maps selected by Ischircoff show quite clearly the preponderance of the Greek element in that country. We have reproduced these maps in facsimile with a brief descriptive comment, adding a few conclusions on the historical aspect and an ethnological summary in which we have attempted to array all other reliable evidence on the subject. We hope we have succeeded in writing *sine ira et studio*, and we leave the facts thus marshalled to speak for themselves.

J. S. M.

December 22nd, 1919   M. G. C.

NOTE.—All the maps in this volume appear also in Rizoff's book, with the exception of the map showing the Greek claim in Thrace and the map of Cvijic which, however, is also based on Bulgarian data. Nineteen of the forty maps given by Rizoff are reproduced in facsimile while the four sketch maps at the end of the volume give the substance of maps 32-40 in Rizoff. The remainder have been omitted either as more or less irrelevant (e.g., a map of the "Contested Zone" in Macedonia) or in order not to multiply evidence unnecessarily. The only omission which calls for a word of comment is that of the three ethnological maps of Panslavist inspiration which Rizoff reproduces. These are the maps prepared by M. F. Mirkowitsch for the Slav Exhibition of Moscow in 1867, the map of the Bohemian Professor Erben (1868) which, according to Rizoff himself, is not original, but based on earlier maps, including that of Mirkowitsch, and finally the map of the Slavonic Beneficent Society of Petrograd (1890). The first two maps, as a matter of fact, admit a Greek preponderance in Thrace but drive a Bulgarian wedge through the centre of the province right up to the walls of "Tsarigrad." The map of the Slavonic Beneficent Society, which Rizoff commends for "its authenticity, accuracy and impartiality" marks almost everything as Bulgarian, including the southern tip of the Gallipoli Peninsula and half the Island of Thasos.

These propagandist maps cancel, and are cancelled by, the parallel productions on the Greek side, such as the map of Bianconi (1877), and the "ethnocratical" map drawn by Kiepert for the Athenian "Society for the propagation of Greek letters" in 1878, which refuse to recognize the existence of Bulgarian agglomerations anywhere south of the Balkan Mountains.

Part I.

HISTORICAL.

I.

THE MAPS OF FREEMAN.*

These four maps from the "Historical Geography of Europe" of Professor E. A. Freeman (3rd Edition by Professor J. B. Bury, 1903), published by Longmans, Green, & Co., illustrate :—

(1.) The period of Czar Simeon (XXXIV).

(2.) The period of Czar Samuel (XXXV).

(3.) The Byzantine domination, when Bulgarian independence had ceased to exist and Bulgaria had become a province of the Byzantine Empire (XXXVIII).

(4.) The reign of Czar Kaloyan (XXXIX).

* Our historical survey begins only with the arrival of the Bulgarians in the Balkan Peninsula. We have thought it unnecessary to dwell on the centuries of Greek colonization in Thrace which preceded it. As early as the seventh century B.C. a belt of Greek cities encompassed the coasts of Thrace, from Abdera and Maronea on the Ægean, to Sozoupolis and Messembria on the Euxine. Through the influence of these cities, the interior of the country had become by the early Christian era so thoroughly Hellenized, that Albert Dumont in his epigraphical tour of Thrace could find only seven inscriptions in another language than Greek, all these being Latin inscriptions on the graves of legionaries, to which in most cases a Greek translation was appended. "All other inscriptions" he adds "are in Greek, even the most barbarous, even those which have the evident stamp of rusticity" (cf. his "Mélanges d'Archéologie et d'Épigraphie," Paris, 1892).

SOUTH EASTERN
EUROPE
C. 910

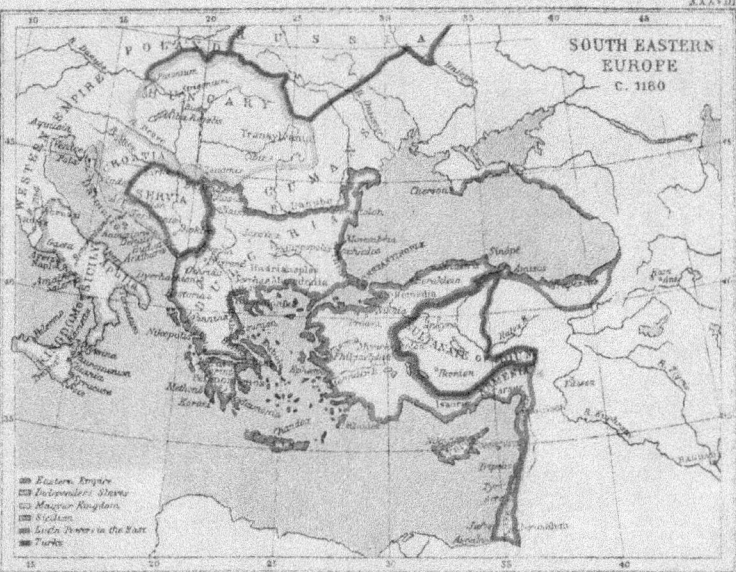

SOUTH EASTERN
EUROPE
C. 1180

SOUTH EASTERN
EUROPE
C. 1000

SOUTH EASTERN
EUROPE
C. 1210

2 – 8 THE MAPS OF ZLATARSKI.

2

BULGARIA UNDER ASPARUCH AND TERVEL.

This map illustrates the earliest Bulgarian settlement within the Balkan Peninsula. About the middle of the seventh century the Bulgarians under their " khan " Asparuch crossed the Danube from Bessarabia, and in 679 a Treaty concluded with the Byzantine Emperor Constantine Pogonatus confirmed them in the possession of the country between the Danube and the Balkan mountains. Under Asparuch's successor Tervel (701-718), the westward frontier of Bulgaria was advanced at the expense of the Avars, while the Treaty of 716 with the Byzantine Empire added to his realm the Zagora territory to the south of the Balkan range.

Bulgarien
zur Zeit des
Asparuch und Tervel
2. Hälfte des VII. u. Anfang
des VIII. Jahrhunderts.

Grenzwall
Grenze
Asparuch
Tervel

SCALE
0   50   100   150   200 KM

BULGARIA UNDER KRUM AND OMURTAG.

The interval between the death of Tervel and the accession of Krum is chiefly noteworthy for the nine Bulgarian campaigns of the Emperor Constantine Copronymus, as a result of which the frontier of Bulgaria was pushed back to the Balkans.

The first half of the reign of Krum (802-814) was taken up with warfare against the Avars. In the course of this the Bulgarian dominions expanded to the north as far as the Theiss. In 809 Krum invaded the Byzantine Empire and captured Sardica (Sofia), and in 811 he defeated and slew in battle the Emperor Nicephorus I. Two years later he ravaged Thrace and appeared before Constantinople, but in 814 he was routed by Leo V. near Messembria, and his son Omurtag (814-831) concluded a 30 years truce which restored the Zagora to Bulgaria.

Bulgarien

zur Zeit des

Krum und Omurtag

Anfang des IX. Jahrhunderts.

SCALE

UNGARN

TRANSYLVANIEN

RUMÄNIEN

BUKAREST

SERBIEN

BOSNIEN

HERZEGOWINA

MONTENEGRO
CETINJE

BULGARIEN

SOFIA

PHILIPPOPEL

ADRIANOPEL

TÜRKEI

CONSTANTINOPEL

MARMARA MEER

MAZEDONIEN

GRIECHENLAND

SALONIK

ÄGÄISCHES MEER

EUROPÄISCHES MEER

EPIRUS

SCHWARZES MEER

Grenzwall

Grenze

4

BULGARIA UNDER PRESSIAM AND BORIS I.

This map, with the Bulgarian expansion into Macedonia which it shows, is based on " the hypothesis which cannot be proved that the Bulgarians had succeeded in annexing the Slavonic tribes to the west of Thessalonica " (cp. Bury, " Eastern Roman Empire," page 372).

Zlatarski asserts that these conquests of Pressiam were confirmed by the Treaty concluded by the Byzantine Empire in 864 with his successor Boris I. (853-888). There is, however, no evidence whatsoever of any such Treaty.

The Treaty of 865, on the occasion of the conversion of Boris to Christianity, only provided for the cession to Bulgaria of an uninhabited stretch of territory adjoining the Zagora.

5

BULGARIA UNDER SIMEON AND PETER.

By the end of the ninth century the conquests of the Magyars and Patzinakitai in Transylvania and Wallachia had made the Danube the northward frontier of Bulgaria. Within the limits, however, of the Balkan Peninsula proper the reign of Simeon (893–927) marks the culmination of the first Bulgarian Empire. Victorious in the great battle of Achelous, he appeared, like Krum before him, under the impregnable walls of Constantinople, where he had himself crowned "Czar and autocrat of all the Bulgars and Greeks." The Serbian Princes became his vassals and his armies over-ran Macedonia and Albania. He was unable, however, to consolidate his conquests, and under his grandson (Boris II.) Bulgaria, terribly weakened by the invasions of Russians under Sviatoslav, was reduced to a Byzantine province by the Emperor John Tzimisces (971).

Zartum Bulgarien

nach dem Tode des

Zar Simeon

927. Jahr.

SCALE

0   50   100   150   200 KM

BULGARIA UNDER SAMUEL.

On the death of John Tzimisces (976) a revolutionary movement broke out in Bulgaria under the leadership of the four sons of the Bulgarian count Shishman. The youngest of these, Samuel, was soon left in undivided power through the death of two of his brothers in battle and the murder of the third by his own orders. The centre of gravity of his monarchy was not in Danubian Bulgaria but in Macedonia, and his capital moved from Sofia to Presba and finally to Ochrida.

The last two decades of the tenth century and the first two of the eleventh are taken up with the great duel for supremacy in the Balkans between Samuel and the Emperor Basil II. ("the Bulgar slayer"). In 1018, after 37 years of devastating warfare, Basil entered Samuel's capital and destroyed his Empire. For 168 years (1018-1186) Bulgaria ceased to be an independent State.

Reich
des
Zar Samuel
zum 996. Jahre

UNGARN

TRANSSYLVANIEN

RUMÄNIEN

SERBIEN

BULGARIEN

MACEDONIEN

BOSNIEN

MONTENEGRO

HERZOGOWINA

EPIRUS

GRIECHENLAND

TÜRKEI

SCHWARZES MEER

MARMARA MEER

ÄGÄISCHES MEER

EUBOEISCHES MEER

DOBRUDSCHA

BELGRAD · SOFIA · BUKAREST · PHILIPPOPOL · ADRIANOPEL · CONSTANTINOPEL · SALONIK · JASI · GALAZ

SCALE
0   50   100   150   200 Km

BULGARIA UNDER ASEN I. AND KALOYAN.

In 1186 two brothers of Vlach origin, Peter and John Asen, raised the standard of revolt at Trnovo. John was proclaimed Czar, and, with Serbian and Kuman assistance, succeeded in establishing his rule from the Danube to the Balkans.

Under his successor Kaloyan, who was crowned " King of Bulgaria and Wallachia," by a cardinal sent to Trnovo by Innocent III., the Bulgarian frontier was advanced southwards at the expense of the Latin States which had been formed after the capture of Constantinople by the Crusaders in 1204.

Bulgarien
zur Zeit des
Assen I. und Kalojan
Ende des XII. und Anfang
des XIII. Jahrhunderts.

SCALE

Assen I.

Kalojan

BULGARIA UNDER JOHN ASEN II.

The second Bulgarian Empire reached its zenith under John Asen II. (1218-1241) as the Empire of Omurtag's line had culminated under Simeon. Victorious at the Battle of Klokotinitza (1230) over the Despot of Epirus, Theodore Angelus, who had annexed to his dominions the territories of the Latin Kingdom of Macedonia, he made himself master (to quote a famous inscription in the Church of the Forty Martyrs at Trnovo) of "all lands from Adrianople to Durazzo—the Greek, the Albanian and the Serbian land."

Zlatarski asserts that Theodore's brother Manuel ruled over the territory coloured with a lighter pink on this map, as a vassal of the Bulgarian Czar. There is, however, no conclusive evidence of such acknowledgment of Bulgarian suzerainty by Manuel; on the contrary, his coins show that he assumed the Imperial title.

Bulgarisches Reich zur Zeit des Zar Joan Assen II. nach dem 1230 Jahre.

BULGARIA AFTER 1355.

This map shows Bulgaria on the eve of the Turkish Conquest.

After the death of John Asen II. in 1241 the second Bulgarian Empire rapidly declined. In 1246 the Nicæan Emperor, John Vatatzes, reconquered Macedonia, and the battle of Berrhœ (1257) drove the Bulgarians out of Thrace, which they never again occupied during the Middle Ages.

In 1330 the defeat of Czar Michael at Velbužd by the Serb King, Stephen Urosh III., reduced Bulgaria to dependence on the growing Serbian Empire. Under Ivan Alexander (1331–1371) the territory of Vidin was detached from the kingdom of Trnovo and became an independent principality, while a nobleman named Dobrotitsch proclaimed himself "Czar" in the "Primorie" or Dobrudja. The principalities of Verbužd and Prilep shown on the map opposite were constituted out of the territories of the Serbian Empire after the death of Stephen Dushan. Zlatarski affects to regard these as Bulgarian states. However, Jireček has conclusively shown that Ivan Dragasch who ruled in Velbužd was a Serb, while our astonishment at finding the famous Kraljević Marko of Prilep described by Zlatarski as " the wonderfully praised hero of the national poetry of Bulgaria" only disappears when we remember that Bulgarian historians have already proved to their own satisfaction that Homer, Orpheus and Alexander the Great were all full-blooded Bulgarians.

Bulgaria took no part in the South Slavonic confederation against the Turks which met with disaster on the field of Kosovo in 1389. This, however, did not prevent Sultan Murad II. from invading Bulgaria two years later, and by 1398 the Turks had reduced the whole country to complete subjection.

Bulgarische Länder

nach

1355.

Legende:

- Königreich Tirnowo
- " " Widin
- Fürstentum Welbujd (Küstendil)
- Königreich Prilep
- Fürstentum Primorié (am Rande des Meeres)

SCALE

A Few Conclusions.

BEFORE drawing any conclusions from the foregoing maps and brief recapitulation of the salient facts of medieval Balkan history, it is necessary to emphasise two points.

The first is the extreme difficulty throughout the period of tracing the frontiers of the various States with any real precision. Data for this purpose are very scanty and have to be constantly supplemented by hypotheses more or less incapable of proof. This difficulty, however, is constantly slurred over by Zlatarski. We have seen that his delimitation of Bulgaria under Pressiam and Boris I. is based on such a hypothesis. The same obtains for his maps of Bulgaria under Simeon and Samuel.

There is no doubt that Simeon's armies repeatedly over-ran Macedonia and Albania, but we have no indication of how far these provinces definitely became parts of his Empire. For instance, the Byzantine chroniclers mention as the first act of his successor an unsuccessful invasion of Macedonia. Of the peace treaty which followed this war we know only that it provided for a marriage alliance between the Bulgarian and Byzantine courts. There is not a word in the chroniclers to back up Zlatarski's assertion that it secured for Bulgaria the territories invaded by Simeon. Similarly of Samuel, we know only the range of his expeditions which reached as far as the Peloponnese to the South and Adrianople to the East; we have no precise indication of how far his writ ran at any given moment.

As Finlay remarks of this very period, "the territories of the two monarchs ran into one another in a very irregular form." All these irregularities, however, are smoothed away on Zlatarski's map.

The second point to be emphasised is that it constitutes an interpretation of the past in terms of the present to see in nationality the essence of these medieval Balkan States. Zlatarski is as justified in seeing in the Empire of John Asen II. the realisation of Bulgarian national unity as an English historian would be in deducing from the conquests of Henry II. and Henry V. the presence of an English population in northern and western France.

To quote Finlay once more, the dominions of both Basil and Samuel "were inhabited by a variety of races, in different states of civilisation, bound together by few sympathies and no common attachment to national institutions."

It is noteworthy in this connection that no Bulgarian sovereign after Simeon contented himself with the title of ruler of the Bulgarians. The "Czars of the Bulgarians and autocrats of the Greeks" of Simeon's house were succeeded two centuries later by the Asenid "Czars of Wallachia and Bulgaria."

After these two reservations, certain deductions are possible from the maps of Zlatarski. It will be noted in the first place that Salonica, on his own showing, has never formed part of any Bulgarian State. Local tradition, indeed, and ecclesiastical art have preserved the legend of how St. Demetrius slew Czar Kaloyan with his lance as he was besieging the great city of which the Saint was the patron and defender.

Similarly, Zlatarski's maps admit that the Chalcidic Peninsula and Eastern Macedonia never came under Bulgarian rule throughout this period. The town of Seres alone twice passed for a short time into Bulgarian hands. Captured for the first time in 1206 by Kaloyan, who burnt it to the ground and deported its inhabitants, it fell once more into Bulgarian hands after the battle of Klokotinitza (1230), only to be lost again a dozen years later.

Finally, with respect to Thrace, the evidence of these maps is decisive. Only during a period of 17 years under John Asen II. in the course of seven centuries did the frontiers of Bulgaria reach the Ægean and include Adrianople. This occupation occurred at a time when the Greek populations of Thrace were inclined to turn to Bulgaria for assistance against the Latin Emperors established in Constantinople by the Fourth Crusade, and an alliance had been concluded against the latter between John Asen II. and the Nicæan Emperor. We possess, moreover, contemporary evidence as to the population of Thrace during the period of the Latin conquest. Villehardouin invariably refers to the inhabitants of the country as "grieu" or "grex." He explicitly mentions as inhabited by Greeks, Dimos (Demotika), Archadiople (Lulé-Burgas), Andrenople (Adrianople), Phinepople (Philippopolis), Rodestoc (Rodosto) and Messinople (Gumuldjina). There is only one reference to Bulgarian inhabitants "a long day's journey" from Messinople in the mountains to the north, probably in the district now called Achi-tchelembi.

After the death of John Asen II., Bulgaria never again obtained a foothold in Thrace. At the Turkish Conquest, the Byzantine frontier with Bulgaria ran along the Balkan range, and the Turkish administrative divisions in recognition of this fact only conferred the name of Boulgar-ili on the territory north of the Balkans, everything to the south of it being called " Roum-ili." A " firman " of 1455 further recognized Greek as an official language in Thrace, alongside of Turkish.

Ethnological data for the first four and a half centuries of Turkish domination are scarcely available. Indeed, the very existence of a Bulgarian nation had been forgotten in Western Europe. Voltaire, it will be remembered, used the name of Bulgaria in "Candide" in the sense of a Ruritania or a *Weissnichtwo*. It was not till 1844 that Cyprien Robert recalled to the mind of Europe the existence of an actual Bulgarian people. The earliest ethnographer of the Balkans with an adequate scientific equipment was, as Ischirkoff points out, Ami Boué, whose map is here given.

THE MAP OF AMI BOUÉ (1847).

This German geologist of French extraction is the author of two works on the Balkans, "La Turquie d'Europe" (1840) and a " Recueil d'Itineraires dans la Turquie d'Europe" (1854). In the former (Vol. II, p. 20) he writes as follows of Thrace : " The Greeks occupy, in the first place, the entire Southern plain of Thrace and the coasts of the Black Sea. They are to be found in the Tekir-Dagh, along the banks of the Maritza, below Adrianople and within this great city itself, as also in Philippopolis and Eski-Zagora. Intermingled with Bulgars and Asiatics they form the population to the south of Rhodope, throughout the breadth of Chalcidice and at Seres and Salonica."

The map on the opposite page first appeared in Berghaus' " Physikalischer Atlas " (1847).

Ethnographische Karte des OSMANISCHEN REICHS europäischen Theils und von GRIECHENLAND

Gotha, bei J. Perthes 1847

10

THE MAP OF LEJEAN (1861).

This map is taken from the " Ethnographie de la Turquie d'Europe " published by G. Lejean, a French Vice-Consul in 1861, as a supplement to the geographical Review " Petermann's Mitteilungen." On page 14 of this treatise it is pointed out that the broadest stretch of territory inhabited by Greeks in the European portion of the Turkish Empire is that between Hafsa (near Adrianople) and Constantinople, and it is explicitly asserted that the Greeks, while a minority in Constantinople itself, form the majority of the population throughout the European hinterland of the capital.

A. SOUCHE INDO GERMANIQUE

SLAVES

Serbes *(Monténégro, Herzégovine, Bosnie, &c.)*

Bulgares *(Bulgarie, &c.)*

Russes *(Malo-Russes, Cosaques, Lipovans, &c.)*

Dalmates

GERMAINS

Allemands

GRÉCO-LATINS

Grecs

Roumains

Tzinzares

Skipetars

B. SOUCHE OUGRO TARTAR

Turcs

Turkomans-Yuruks

Tartares *(Nogaïs Cabenssiens)*

Magyars *(Hongrois Széklers, &c)*

C. SOUCHE SÉMITIQUE

Juifs *(surtout dans Roumélie)*

Arabes *(gitanos)*

Arnaoutins *(dans les villes)*

D. RACES DIVERSES

Tsiganes *(surtout dans Roumanie, nomades en Bulgarie & en Albanie &c)*

CARTE ETHNOGRAPHIQUE
DE LA
TURQUIE D'EUROPE
ET DES ÉTATS VASSAUX AUTONOMES
PAR G. LEJEAN.

MER ÉGÉE

MER DE MARMARA

Longitude Est de Greenwich

Longitude Est de Paris

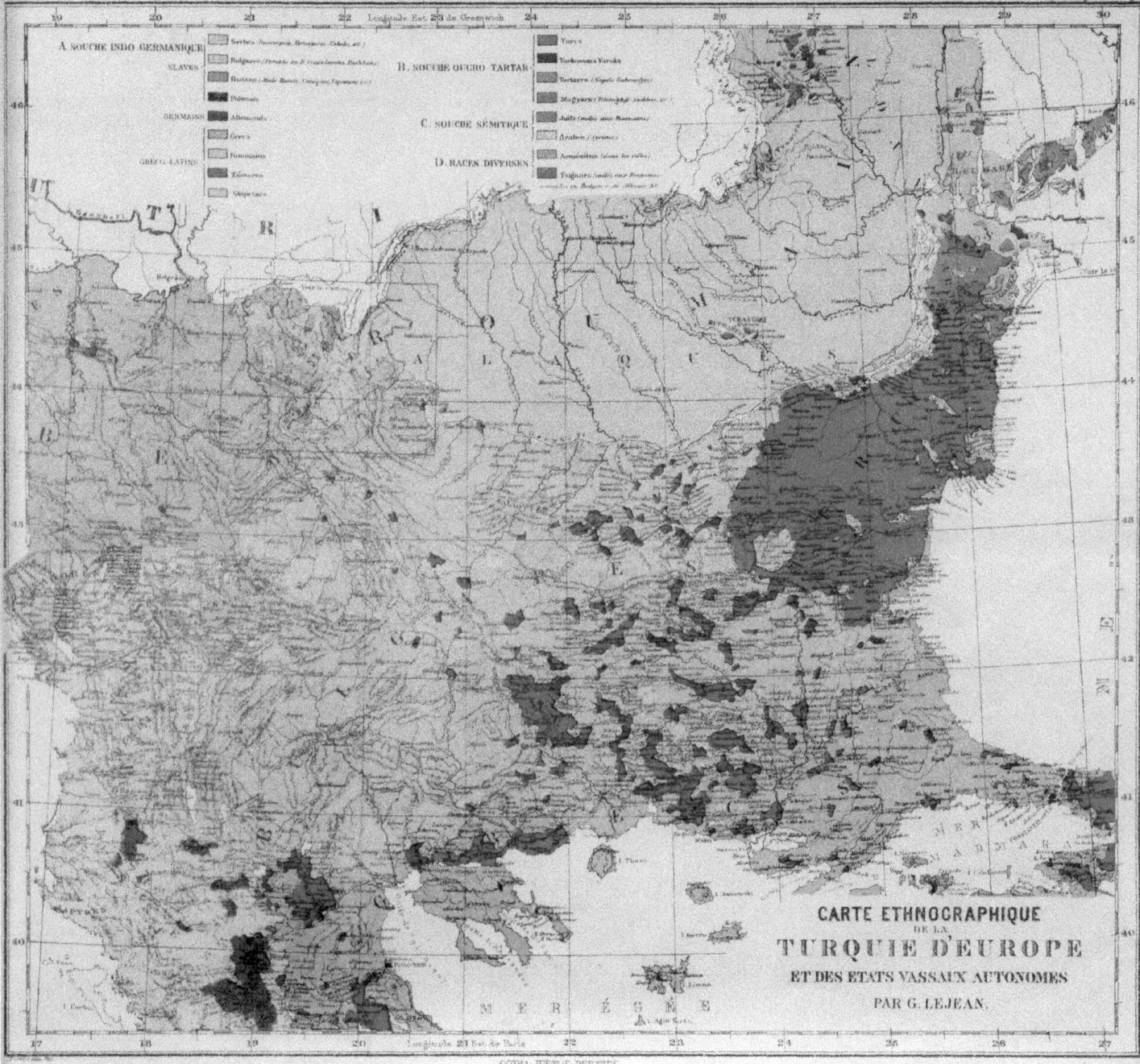

GOTHA: JUSTUS PERTHES

THE MAP OF MACKENZIE AND IRBY (1867).

This map is the work of two English ladies, who, after extensive travels in the Balkans, published in 1867 a volume on " The Turks, the Greeks and the Slavons." " In Thrace," say the authors, " Adrianople may be taken as a boundary city for the Bulgarians." A second edition of this book appeared ten years later with a preface by Mr. Gladstone.

MOLDAVIA

Buda-Pesth

Temesvar

WALACHIA

Bucharest

Danube

Kustendje

BLACK SEA

Varna

BOSNIA

Belgrade

PRINCIPALITY OF
SERVIA

Kragujevac

Widin

BULGARIA

Mustapha

Bourgas

Sarajevo
Bosna Serai

Nish

Sophia

Philippopolis

RUMELIA

ADRIATIC SEA

Ragusa

Antivari

Scutari

Durazzo

Ochrida

Monastir

Salonica

Mt Athos

CONSTANTINOPLE

SEA of
MARMORA

AEGEAN
SEA

Smyrna

GREECE

MAP
of the
SOUTH SLAVONIC
COUNTRIES.

Scale of English Miles.

Railways thus ----

NOTE

Southern Slavs.

I. In Turkey.		
Bulgarians extend from Cattaro to Kustendje		2,253,802
Croato Serbs		2,583,000
3. In Montenegro from 120,000 to	196,000	

II. In Austria.		
Croats Serbs		2,357,802
Slovenes		1,151,864
Bulgarians		21,847

Explanation of Colours.

Serbian	Bulgarian
Bulgarian	light green
Turkish	red
Greek	blue
Albanian	yellow
Roumans	
Turk-colon Servian friends	grey
German	purple

W. & A. K. Johnston, Edinburgh.

12.

THE MAP OF ELISÉE RECLUS (1876).

This is taken from the famous "Nouvelle Geographie Universelle" published in 1876. On page 161 of the first volume of this work appears the following passage : " The population of the villages and plains of Thrace consists almost exclusively of Greeks. They are the occupants and cultivators of the soil. By a remarkable contrast, precisely opposite Asia, within the section of the Balkan Peninsula where the Turks have been longest settled, the Greeks have their largest ethnological domain, exclusive of the Pindus region. There they occupy not only the coast but all the interior of the country. Apart from the large towns and occasional Bulgarian villages, all Eastern Thrace is theirs. From the Bosphorus to Adrianople, from the Dardanelles to the Gulf of Burgas, it is all Hellenic territory."

Nº 24. Nouvelle Géographie Universelle
Hachette et Cie Paris.

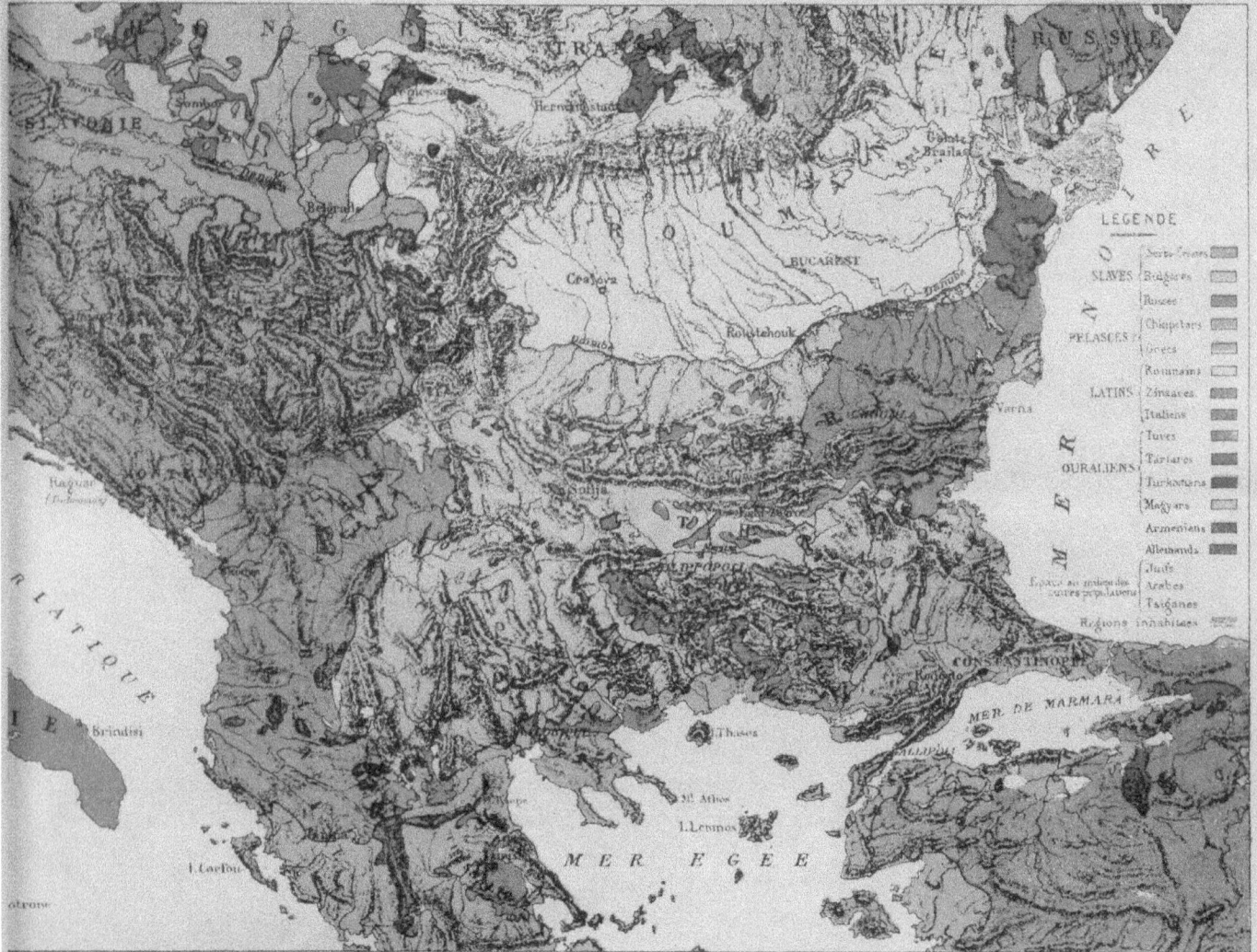

LEGENDE

SLAVES	Serbo-Croates
	Bulgares
	Russes
PÉLASGES	Chiopetars
	Grecs
LATINS	Roumains
	Zinzares
	Italiens
OURALIENS	Turcs
	Tartares
	Turkomans
	Magyars
	Arméniens
	Allemands
	Juifs
	Arabes
	Tsiganes
	Régions inhabitées

Espacé au milieu des autres populations

d'après Lejean, Kanitz, de Goering

Imp. Erhard Frères, Rue Fontaine

NB. Cette carte ne peut avoir qu'une valeur tout approximative, la plupart
des populations de races et de langues diverses sont entremêlées et non superposées.

13.

THE MAP OF KIEPERT (1876).

This map of the great German geographer enjoyed the distinction of being accepted by the Berlin Congress as a basis for its deliberations on the frontiers of Bulgaria and Eastern Rumelia.

ETHNOGRAPHISCHE ÜBERSICHT DES EUROPÄISCHEN ORIENTS

zusammengestellt von H. KIEPERT, Berlin im Mai 1876.

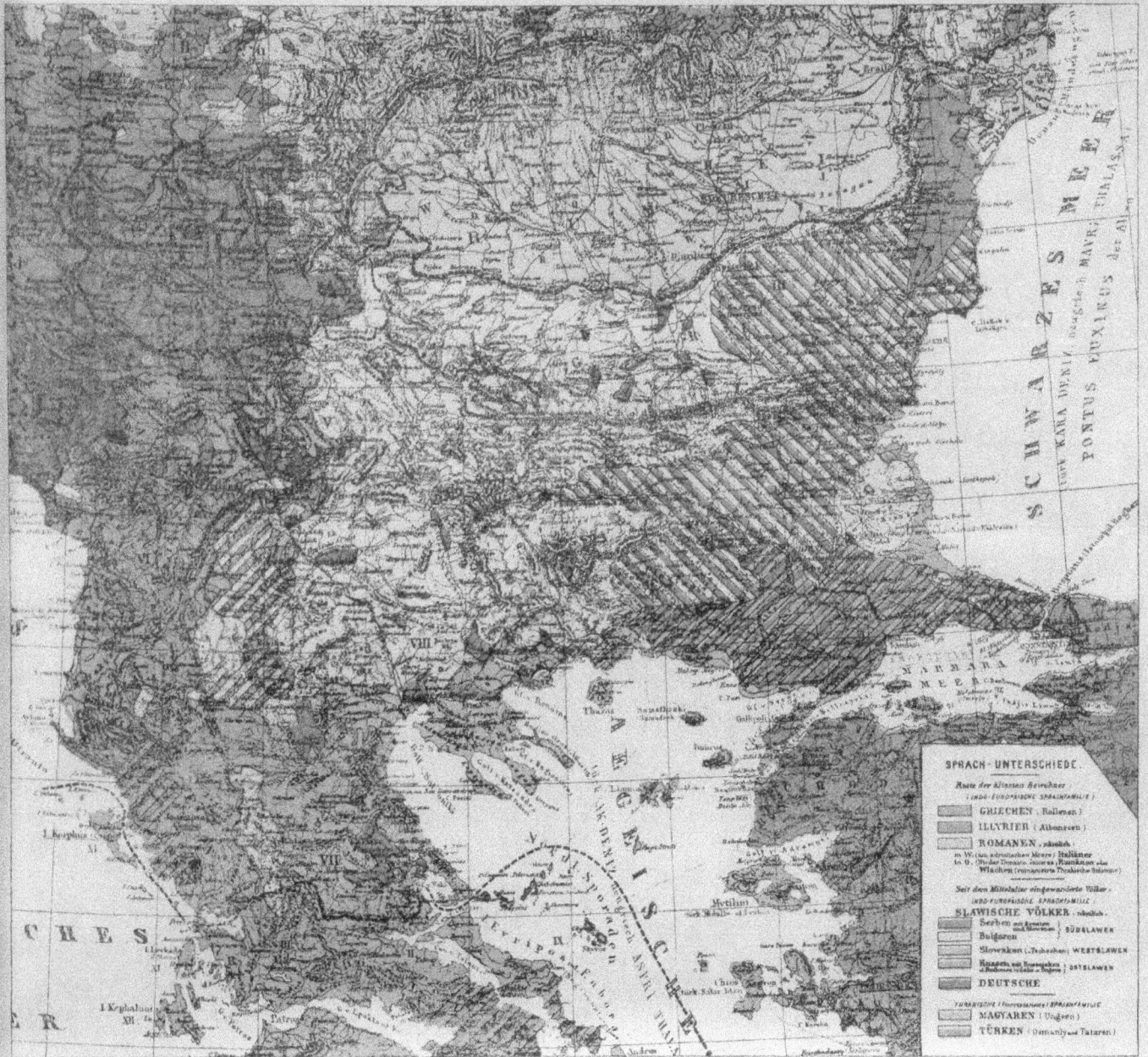

13.

SCHWARZES MEER

PONTUS EUXINUS der Alten

SPRACH-UNTERSCHIEDE.

Reste der ältesten Bewohner
(INDO-EUROPÄISCHE SPRACHFAMILIE)

GRIECHEN (Hellenen)

ILLYRIER (Albanesen)

ROMANEN, nämlich

im W. (am adriatischen Meere) Italiäner
in O. (W. der Donau) Istroren, Rumänen oder
Wlachen (romanisirte Thrakische Stämme)

Seit dem Mittelalter eingewanderte Völker
INDO-EUROPÄISCHE SPRACHFAMILIE

SLAWISCHE VÖLKER : nämlich

Serben mit Bosniern und Slowenzen   SÜDSLAWEN
Bulgaren
Slowaken (Tschechen)   WESTSLAWEN
Russen mit Russniaken u. Bulgaren u. Russen   OSTSLAWEN

DEUTSCHE

TURKISCHE (URALISCHE) SPRACHFAMILIE

MAGYAREN (Ungern)

TÜRKEN (Osmanly und Tataren)

14.

THE MAP OF SYNVET (1877).

The author of this map was for many years a teacher at the Lycée Ottoman in Constantinople, and published a " Table Ethnographique de la Turquie d'Europe " in 1877. In this he puts the total Greek population of Thrace, exclusive of Constantinople but including Eastern Rumelia, at 380,000. Omitting Eastern Rumelia, for which he gives 68,000 Greeks, we have thus, according to Synvet, 312,000 Greeks in the Vilayet of Adrianople.

CARTE ETHNOGRAPHIQUE
de la
TURQUIE d'EUROPE
par
A. SYNVET

I. District de Constantinople II. Vilayet d'Edirné III. Vilayet de Touna et de Sophia
IV. Vilayet de Bosna et de Hersek V. Vilayet de Monastir VI. Vilayet de Iania
VII. Vilayet de Selanik VIII. Vilayet de Giaiñ IX. Vilayet de Bezair-Bahri - Séfid

Grécs-Bulgares Grecs Musulmans Bulgares

Serbo-Croates Roumains Albanais

MER NOIRE

MER DE MARMARA

CONSTANTINOPLE

VARNA

15.

THE MAP OF CVIJIC (1913).

This map, which appeared in " Petermann's Mitteilungen " in 1913, is based on material supplied to the author, one of the most distinguished of living geographers, by M. Karajovov, Bulgarian Consul in Adrianople. It clearly establishes on the basis of Bulgarian statistics that south of Adrianople the Bulgarian element in Thrace is everywhere a hopeless minority. It is, however, occasionally unfair to the Greeks. It marks for instance, as preponderantly Turkish the Kirk-Kilissé district where the Greek element, represented on this map by a small enclave, is admitted to be the most numerous by official Turkish statistics. The " Gagausen " represented on Cvijic's map with the Turkish colour are Greeks who speak Turkish. They are found chiefly round Hafsa and are estimated at a little over 3,000.

ETHNOGRAPHISCHE KARTE DER BALKANHALBINSEL

Von Prof. Dr. J. Cvijic

LEGENDE

- Griechen
- Türken, Tataren und Gagausen
- Orthodoxe Islamisierte Pomaken
- Orthodoxe

16.

THE MAP OF THE BULGARIAN PROFESSORS.

The map on the opposite page is part of a map of the Balkan Peninsula drawn up by five Bulgarian professors in 1915 and published in " Petermann's Mitteilungen."   The part here reproduced is the work of Prof. L. Miletisch who is stated to have derived his data for Eastern Thrace from an exhaustive investigation of the existing literature on the subject and from the accounts of Bulgarian refugees, while well acquainted personally with the Western half of the province.   A comparison of this map with any of the preceding will explain the comment of the German geographer Otto Maull that " even in the ethnographical literature of south-eastern Europe it is very difficult to find anything to compare with what the coalition of Bulgarian ethnographers has here done in its effort to annihilate the Greek element, especially in Thrace."

DAS BULGARENTUM AUF DER BALKANHALBINSEL IM JAHRE 1912

Von Prof. Dr. A. Ischirkoff unter Mitwirkung von Prof. Dr. L. Miletitsch, Prof. Dr. B. Zoneff, Prof. J. Ivanoff, Prof. Dr. St. Romanski

LEGENDE
- Griechen
- Turken
- Bulgaren
- Serben

An Ethnological Summary.

These ethnological maps, drawn from so many diverse sources, all agree in revealing at a glance the preponderantly Hellenic character of Thrace. Their evidence, conclusive as it must appear, can be corroborated in other ways.

It was no doubt mainly on ethnical grounds that the Ambassadorial Conference held at Constantinople in 1876-1877, having proposed the establishment of an autonomous Bulgarian province tributary to the Porte, drew its southern frontier north of Adrianople and along the Arda river—a line very closely approximating to that originally proposed by M. Venizelos in the Greek interest.

It is also worth recording that at the Berlin Congress Lord Salisbury criticised the treaty of San Stefano for handing over to Bulgaria " provinces as Greek as Crete," among which he explicitly mentioned Thrace, though even that treaty left Adrianople outside the Bulgarian frontiers. These facts effectively dispose of the allegation that the present weakness of the Bulgarian element in Thrace is due to an expulsion of 300,000 Thracian Bulgarians by the Turkish authorities, just before the Russo-Turkish War.

That the Bulgarian element in Thrace is to-day a negligible quantity, save only for a narrow belt of territory along the old Turco-Bulgarian frontier to which Greece has never laid claim, can be conclusively established in a variety of ways. In the first place two detailed censuses of Thrace are available. The first is an official Turkish estimate which appeared in the " Salnameh " or Almanack of the Vilayet of Adrianople in 1894. The second was drawn up by the Oecumenical Patriarchate in 1912. The figures in both which bear on the parts of Thrace claimed by Greece are reproduced in an appendix. Both agree in putting the Greek element first, with the Bulgarian a bad third.

Again, the Firman of 1870 instituting the Bulgarian Exarchate, provided for the transfer from the jurisdiction of the Patriarchate to that of the Exarchate of any diocese in which two-thirds of the Christian population should vote for such a transfer. Rizoff emphasises the value of these plebiscites in Macedonia as a vindication of the Bulgarian character of that country. It is only fair to draw the opposite conclusion from the fact that no Bulgarian bishop has ever been installed in any part of Thrace. However, the most conclusive piece of evidence is afforded by the electoral compact concluded in 1912 by the delegates of the Greek and Bulgarian populations of the Empire with a view to their representation in the Ottoman Parliament. Under the joint auspices of the Bulgarian Exarchate and the Oecumenical Patriarchate it was agreed that the electoral distribution in Thrace, " on the basis of the duly certified numerical strength of the two nations " (the words of the Protocol) should be seven Greek deputies and one Bulgarian. MM. Gueshoff and Tsokoff in a Memorandum to the Peace Conference have attempted to interpret this as a concession to the Greek populations of Constantinople and the Dardanelles region, to which Bulgaria has never laid claim. The Protocol, however, specified that three Greek deputies were to be returned along with one Bulgarian in the Vilayet of Adrianople minus the Sandjak of Gallipoli, i.e., in Thrace, exclusive of the parts referred to by MM. Gueshoff and Tsokoff. An additional article, moreover, stipulated that " should the Bulgarians fail to return their one deputy, the Greeks undertake to bring about the resignation of one of their own deputies elected at Adrianople or Kirk-Kilisse, and to exert all their forces to bring about the election of a Bulgarian deputy in his place." As a matter of fact, no Bulgarian deputy was returned. Similarly in 1913, after the annexation of Western Thrace to Bulgaria, the deputies returned to the Bulgarian Sobranje for this province were all Moslems, while Eastern Thrace again returned three Greek deputies to the Ottoman Parliament and not a single Bulgarian.

The Bulgarians would strengthen their case in Thrace by reckoning in as Bulgarians the " Pomaks " or Moslems of Bulgarian speech, computed by MM. Gueshoff and Tsokoff at 95,000, though even Professor Ischirkoff, one of Rizoff's collaborators, has admitted that " their new religion, while sparing their language and many of their traditions, has completely destroyed their national spirit." (cf. Petermann's Mitteilungen, 1911, Vol. II., page 219.) Similarly, an article by M. A. Strasimiroff in the Sofia newspaper Dnevnik, on July 18th, 1915, urged the necessity of disarming the Pomak populations annexed to Bulgaria by the Treaty of Bucarest on the ground that " the Pomaks, so long as they retain their rifles, consider the Bulgarian régime to be only provisional." It is, however, unnecessary to labour this point here, for the Rhodope uplands, where the Pomaks are concentrated, are in any case left to Bulgaria by the terms of the Peace Treaty. Outside this region even M. Theodoroff only gives 18,000 Pomaks in Thrace.

The Peace Conference, on the other hand, has refused to endorse the argument that the necessities of Bulgarian trade entitle Bulgaria to retain her hold on the Northern Ægean. Bulgaria already possesses in Varna and Burgas two excellent harbours, and, with the freedom of the Straits internationally guaranteed, there is no reason why, in complete disregard of the facts of racial distribution, she should enjoy a privileged position as against the other States which, like her, have only a frontage on the Black Sea. The Greek Government, moreover, in order to deprive the argument of all force, has undertaken to give Bulgaria a commercial right-of-way under the control of the League of Nations to Cavalla or Dedeagatch, and to build at its own expense a railway between this port and the Bulgarian frontier.

The apologists of Bulgaria have also attempted to make capital out of the fact that during the peace negotiations which followed the first Balkan war, the Greek Government supported the claim of Bulgaria, then Greece's ally, to annex, at the expense of Turkey, Adrianople and all Thrace up to the Enos-Midia line. This is taken as a recognition of Bulgarian ethnical rights in that territory. However, M. Venizelos at the time made his position quite clear. Speaking in the Greek Chamber on March 15th, 1913, he said : " Greek populations, and compact Greek populations at that, must of necessity remain under the sovereignty of our allies. There are certain necessities which no man can ignore." Greek aspirations in Thrace were to be deliberately sacrificed to the higher interest of the preservation of the Balkan League. To interpret M. Venizelos' policy in this matter as a recognition of Bulgarian rights is to miss the whole point of it. To-day the higher interest to which Greek aspirations in Thrace were to be sacrificed, is no longer practical politics—through no fault of Greece. " Abiit illud tempus" as Cicero said in an analogous case : " mutata ratio est." In his Memorandum to the Peace Conference M. Venizelos put the matter in a nutshell : " To persist in the same tendency, to wish still to make concessions to Bulgaria would be on my part an act of unhealthy political sentimentalism.

BULGARIA
as proposed by
Ambassadorial Conference
CONSTANTINOPLE
1876

BULGARIA
According to
SAN STEFANO TREATY
1878

BALKAN FRONTIERS
According to
BERLIN TREATY
1878

BALKAN FRONTIERS
According to
BUCHAREST TREATY
1913

An Ethnological Summary—*continued.*

My countrymen would justly disavow me, for such a policy would sacrifice, without any compelling reason, the vital interests of my country for the partial satisfaction of an insatiable neighbour, who would take advantage of it to exterminate the alien populations fallen under his domination and would draw new strength therefrom for a new attack at an opportune moment."

It remains to treat as briefly as possible of the considerable Turkish element in Thrace. It should be noted, in the first place, that in statistics all Moslems, regardless of race, are grouped together as " Turks." Indeed, the " Turkish " element in Thrace is thickest in the highlands of Western Thrace, occupied almost exclusively by Pomak and Achriane mountaineers who hide under conformity to Islam the mystery of their origin.* Moslem preponderance here, however, is irrelevant to an appreciation of Greek claims, for this territory is left to Bulgaria. For the parts of Thrace actually claimed by Greece, Turkish and Greek statistics are agreed in showing a Greek majority (304,537 Greeks and 265,359 Turks in the one case, and 393,515 Greeks and 344,011 Turks in the other).

This majority may not appear overwhelming, but three points should be borne in mind. In the first place, the Turkish element in the country is artificially swollen by an enormous floating population of soldiers and officials recruited from the Anatolian homelands of the race. An illustration will make clear the force of this point. Turkish statistics show that no less than 43,000 inhabitants of Constantinople are persons in Government service. If we multiply this figure by five in order to include their families we have accounted for fully half of the Turkish population of the capital. Something analogous, though in a less degree, obtains throughout Thrace. If we could take into consideration only the permanent and settled population, Greek preponderance in Thrace would be much more striking. It is suggestive in this connection that M. Berl, a publicist sent on a special mission to the country by the French Government a few years before the war, calculates that the Greek element, though only about 35 per cent. of the total population of Thrace,† has in its hands 50 per cent. of the agriculture, 80 per cent. of the industry and 70 per cent. of the trade of the country, besides almost monopolising the liberal professions.

In the second place, a glance at the ethnological maps will show that the relative strength of the Greek and Turkish elements in Thrace has undergone a considerable change, to the disadvantage of the Greek element, since 1877. This is due to the policy inaugurated by Abdul Hamid of attracting Moslem immigrants (Mohadjirs) from former provinces of the Empire, notably Bosnia, Crete and Bulgaria, and settling them in predominantly Christian regions with a view to modifying their ethnological complexion. One estimate puts the number of " Mohadjirs " thus settled in Thrace since the Russo-Turkish War as high as 188,000. Since 1914, this process has been carried one step further by the Young Turkish Government, which has seized the opportunity afforded by the war to deport 120,000 Thracian Greeks from their homes and settle Moslems in their place, not to mention several tens of thousands more driven out and compelled to take refuge in Greece during the spring of the same year. About half of these 120,000 have perished of hunger and privation.‡ The repatriation of those still alive is an act of elementary justice besides being, as the report of the Inter-Allied Commission already referred to points out, " by far the soundest means of restoring prosperity in the country." It is doubtful if after such a repatriation the Turks would have a majority in Thrace, as the Turkish element has also been thinned by the war and epidemics, but, in any case, the majority that counts is surely the pre-war majority, not the majority obtained through deportation and " white massacre." One cannot admit the assassin's claim to step into the shoes of his victim.

Finally, we must ask ourselves which is the element which " plays the music of the Zukunft." In all cases where the future of territories of mixed population is under consideration, a long-sighted view is only possible if we also take into account the tendencies and possibilities presented by the various elements. One cannot ignore such a fact as the strikingly higher rate of increase of the Greek element. The example of Cyprus is there to show that under an administration which does not attempt to control racial growth through massacre, the Greeks increase three times as rapidly as the Turks.‡ Nor can one deny that the Greek element alone possesses the vitality necessary for reconstruction on the ruins of to-day. A distinguished Italian publicist has well expressed the certain facts noted by every careful observer of the Near East. " The Greek people believe that their mission in the East is not yet at an end. Their consciousness of their own superiority, their intellectual gifts, their pride, their aptitude for commerce, and peaceful progress generally, their family organisation, which assigns to women a post of action and direction worthy of them (even the Turks respect Greek women and reserve for them the title of " kokona " or " matron "), their taste for learning, their undying optimism, their inability ever to feel discouragement, their characteristic versatility . . . and their profound knowledge of life constitute a justification of this idea." (Amadori Virgilj, " La questione rumeliota," pp. 51-52.) " In the immobile Orient the Greek nation alone personifies the Western spirit of activity and progress. . . . The Moslems who in this nineteenth century respect and fear Greek nationality while fighting against it, show thereby their respect and at the same time their dread of the invading civilisation of the West." (Ib., page 52.)

And, lastly, may we say a word to those persons who, while anxious to do justice, are reduced to despair by the tangled ethnography of the Balkan region and are inclined to find refuge in mandates and international controls? These expedients of the League of Nations are excellent in their appropriate place and season, but, if applied too indiscriminately, they may become engines of injustice, belying that doctrine of self-determination and majority-rule which supplies the very *raison d'être* of the League. Thrace affords a test of the validity of that doctrine just as much as Transylvania or Bohemia. Minorities, whether large or small, should have every right assured to them, short of the right to deny self-determination to a majority.

To put Thrace, the " largest ethnological domain of the Greek race north of Pindus," as Reclus called it, under the mandate of a Great Power would only mean turning it into a second Crete

The Greek element, already a relative majority numerically and enjoying the higher birth-rate, absolutely preponderant in economic life, and monopolizing such culture as the country possesses, could not fail to assert its preponderance more and more strongly under any civilized government and to press with ever increasing force its plea for the union of Thrace to the Mother Country. The mandatory solution is above all a compromise, and the precedents of Eastern Rumelia and Crete are there to show that the Balkans do not take kindly to such compromises.

---

* The Pomaks have been variously conjectured to be of Bulgarian, primitive Thracian, Armenian Paulician, Tartar, Kurman and Greek origin. The Achrianes may be " sons of Agar " or descendants of the ancient Agrianoi or anything.

† That is inclusive of the parts not claimed by Greece.

‡ These figures are taken from a report of the chief representative of the Inter-Allied Commission in Constantinople, & a communication by M. Venizelos in the " Morning Post " of October 21st.

‡ The Cyprus census of 1910 shows that the Greek element has increased 63% as against a Turkish increase of 21½% since 1881, the year of the first census carried out by the British administration.

18

B U L G A R I A

B L A C K
S E A

Agathupolis
Tyrnovo
Cape Iniada

Mustapha-
Pasha
Kirdjali
Kirk-Kilisse
KIRK-KILISSE Midia
Adrianople
Egri-Dere
Achi-
Tchelembi
Ortakeul
Sultan-
Yeri
ADRIANOPLE
Hafsa
Viza
Lule-Burgas
Dari-Dere
Dimotika
GUMULDJINA
GREECE
Harioupolis
Tchorlu
CHATALJA
Chatalja
Xanthi
Gumuldjina
Sufli
Ouzoum-
Keupru
RODOSTO
Silivri
Constantinople
CONSTANTINOPLE
Kavala
Rodosto
DEDEAGATCH
Malgara
Dedeagatch
Keshan
SEA   OF
THASOS
Enos
GALLIPOLI
Myriophyton
M A R M O R A
SAMOTHRAKI
Gallipoli
IMBROS
Dardanelles

LEMNOS

The dotted red line shows the Greek claim as
originally formulated by M. Venizelos.
The solid line represents the frontier of
Bulgaria as fixed by the Treaty of Neuilly
(November 27th, 1919) and, therefore, the
Northern Boundary of the present
Greek Claim.

Map showing
GREEK CLAIM
IN
THRACE

Limit of Greek Claims
Boundaries of Vilayets
Boundaries of Sandjaks
Boundaries of Kazas

0   5   10   20   30   40   50 MILES

APPENDIX.—STATISTICAL TABLES.

APPENDIX.—STATISTICAL TABLES.—Throughout this book the term "Thrace" has been used in its most usual connotation, so as to exclude both Constantinople on the one hand and the territory of Eastern Rumelia on the other hand, though the limits of Thrace are sometimes extended so as to include both of these. Thrace thus defined corresponds to the old Turkish "vilayet" of Adrianople, made up of the six "Sandjaks" of Gumuldjina, Dedeagatch, Gallipoli, Rodosto, Kirk-Kilissé, and Adrianople, each sub-divided into a varying number of "cazas." We give below the population of those parts of Thrace which the Treaty of Neuilly leaves outside the Bulgarian frontiers, and the political status of which remains to be settled by the Peace Conference. We also give the figures for the adjoining Sandjak of Tchataldja.

OFFICIAL TURKISH STATISTICS OF 1894.

	GREEKS.	MUSULMANS.	BULGARIANS.
Sandjak of Adrianople			
Caza of Adrianople ...	28,256	36,597	9,289
,, Ortakeü ...	10,356	15,671	3,955
,, Ouzoun Kieupru	15,698	13,398	5,473
,, Hafsa ...	5,650	6,830	1,310
,, Demotika ...	16,805	7,504	1,243
	76,765	80,000	21,270
Sandjak of Gumuldjina			
Caza of Gumuldjina ...	8,325	32,676	7,042
Sandjak of Dédéagatch	34,097	28,427	12,899
Sandjak of Gallipoli ...	64,929	25,889	909
Sandjak of Rodosto ...	35,569	41,729	3,430
Sandjak of Kirk-Kilissé			
(Less the Cazas of Tyrnovo and Agathoupolis)...	49,232	40,308	21,221
	268,017	249,039	66,771
The official Turkish Statistics of 1897, published in Constantinople in 1900, give the following numbers for the			
Sandjak of Tchataldja ...	36,520	16,320	5,987
Total ...	304,537	265,359	72,758

GREEK STATISTICS OF 1912.

	GREEKS.	MUSULMANS.	BULGARIANS.
Sandjak of Adrianople			
Caza of Adrianople ...	41,285	44,953	7,000
,, Ortakeüy ...	14,562	15,273	4,060
,, Ouzoun Kieupru	19,197	10,610	5,600
,, Hafsa ...	9,160	8,235	730
,, Demotika ...	22,080	6,315	1,460
	106,284	85,386	18,850
Sandjak of Gumuldjina			
Caza of Gumuldjina ...	9,160	50,000	10,550
Sandjak of Dédéagatch	28,851	46,400	16,738
Sandjak of Gallipoli ...	79,431	32,513	2,000
Sandjak of Rodosto ...	55,570	63,725	2,980
Sandjak of Kirk-Kilissé			
(Less the Cazas of Tyrnovo and Agathoupolis) ...	68,432	49,787	16,725
	338,728	327,911	67,843
Sandjak of Tchataldja	54,787	16,100	
Total ...	393,515	344,011	67,843

SKETCH MAP OF RUSSIAN AND RUMANIAN FRONTIERS

SHOWING NATIONALITIES OF NORTH-WEST RUSSIA.

SWEDEN

Aland Isl.
STOCKHOLM

BALTIC

PETROGRAD

ESTHONIA
Dagö
Oesel
L. Peipus
Walk
L. Pskov
LIVONIA
COURLAND
D.L. Luban
Libau
Olevenhof
KOVNO
Kovno
Vilna
Suwa...
NIemen
Pruzhany
Brest Litovsk
L. Wygonovsk
Pinsk
Pripet
Vistula
WARSAW
POLAND
Cholm
VOLHYNIA
KIEV
Kiev
Dnieper
GALICIA
PODOLIA
Dniester
BUKOVINA
BESSARABIA
KHERSON
Dorna Vatral
Jassy
Prut
Kishinev
Odessa
Galatz
DOBRUJA
BLACK
SEA
Orsova Verciorova
RUMANIA
BUCHAREST
Danube
SERBIA
BULGARIA

GERMANY

AUSTRIA-

HUNGARY

VITEBSK
Dvina
MOHILEV
Moh.-Jev.
MINSK

Boundary agreed on
++++ between Russia and
Central Powers,
March 3, 1918.

Boundary agreed on
••••• between Ukraine and
Central Powers,
Feb. 9, 1918.

Letts

Lithuanians

White Russians

Esths

Boundaries between States

Boundaries of Provinces

Former boundary between
Russia & Poland

Scale of Miles
100 75 50 25 0   100

20.3.18.

Intell. Bureau, Dept. of Infn.

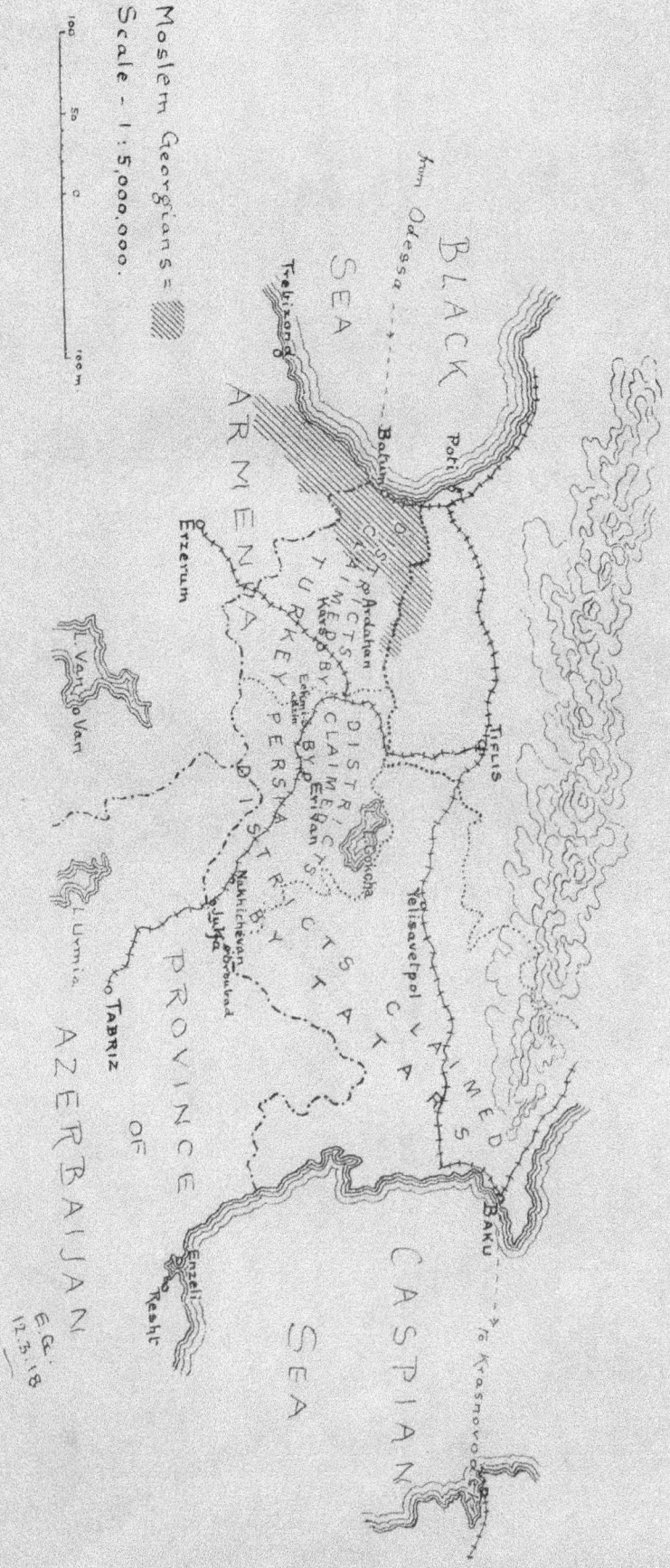

TRANSCAUCASIA

BLACK SEA

from Odessa ....

Trebizond

Poti

Batum

Erzerum

L. Van

L. Urmia

TIFLIS

DISTRICTS CLAIMED BY ARMENIA

DISTRICTS CLAIMED BY TURKEY DISTRICTS CLAIMED BY PERSIA

ARMENIA

Ardahan

Kars

Erivan

Echmiadzin

Nakhichevan

Julfa

TABRIZ

PROVINCE OF AZERBAIJAN

Yelisavetpol

Baku .... to Krasnovodsk

CASPIAN SEA

Enzeli

Resht

E.G.
12.3.18

Moslem Georgians =

Scale - 1:5,000,000.

100   50   0   100 m.

Vienna   R. Danube

STYRIA

CARINTHIA

CARNIOLA   Agram

Triesta

ISTRIA   Fiume

CROATIA

R. Drave

SLAVONIA

R. Save

BOSNIA

DALMATIA

Sebenico

Spalato

Metković

Sarayevli

Mostar

Budapest

HUNGARY

Szegedin   Makó Arad

Zenta

BANAT

Belgrade

R. Teiss

Grosswardein

TRANSYLVANIA

R. Marosh

MARAMURESH

Czernowitz

BUKOVINA

Wooded Carpathians

RUSSIA

R. Dniester

BESSARABIA

R. Pruth

Iassy   Kishinev

R. Sereth

Bender

Galatz

Braila

RUMANIA

Bucarest

Czaful

Kilia Mouth

Sulina

DOBRODJA

Constanza

Mangalia

SERBIA

Snpska Morava

R. Drina

MONTE NEGRO

Cettinje

Grahovo

Risano

Cattaro

Spizza

Dulcigno

R. Bojana

R. Drini

Scutari

ALBANIA

Durazzo

Valona

Argyrokastro

Delvino

Corfu

Parga

Jannina

R. Ibar

Nish

Pirot

Vidin

Rustchuk

Silistria

Tutrakan

Dobritch

Baltchik

Varna

BULGARIA

Sofia

Kiostendil

R. Maritza

Burgas

Adrianople

Kirkilissa

LuleBurgas

Midia

Rodosto

Constantinople

Enos

Dedeagatch

Mt. Golem

CONTESTED ZONE

Dibra

Monastir

L. Ochrida

Tresovo

Vodena

Castoria

Verria

L. Doiran

Strumitza

Nigrita

Serres

Tachyno

Kavala

I. Thasos

Salonika

THESSALY

Larissa

Volo

Patras

MOREA

Athens

PROVISIONAL

ITALY

HUNGARY

Graz

Marburg

Laibach

Zagrab

TRIEST

Fiume

Pola

Szeged

Szabadka

Neusatz

BELGRADE

RUMANIA

Negotin

BULGARIA

Sarajevo

SERBIA

Sofiya

Spalato

Mostar

Nish

MONTENEGRO

Cetinje

Uskub

A L B A N I A

Ochrida
Monastir

SALONICA

Valona

GREECE

A D R I A T I C   S E A

NATIONALITIES

over 95%   50-95%

Italians
Rumanians
Magyars
Germans
Slovenes
Croats
Serbs : Christian
Serbs : Moslem

YUGO-SLAVS

Scale 1 : 1,700,000

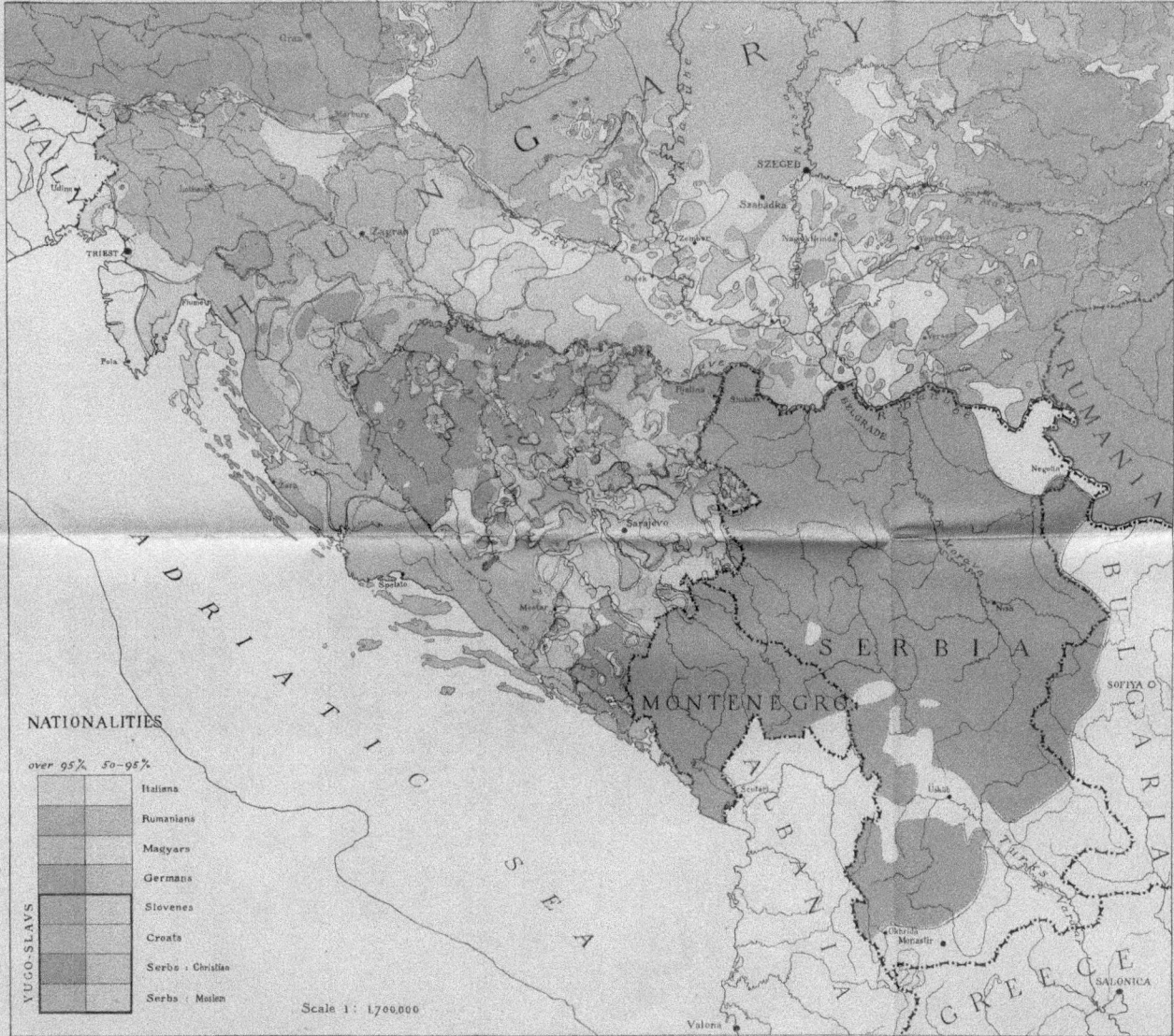

Naval Staff I.D.

YUGO- SLAVIA.

NEW FRONTIERS IN CENTRAL EUROPE & DANUBIAN TERRITORY

Scale of Miles

GERMANY

POLAND
Poland-Russia
(as required by Polish National Council)

Occupied by Poles but
claimed by Czechs

o Warsaw

o Lublin

RUSSIA

UKRANIA

Kiev

Jitomir

Tchernigov

Posen

Silesia

Prague

Bohemia

Olmutz
Prossnitz
Moravia
Brunn

CZECHO-SLOVAKIA

Pressburg

VIENNA

Klagenfurt

Marburg

Laibach

Trieste

Fiume

Gratz

R. Save

YUGO-SLAVIA

Belgrade

HUNGARY

BUDAPEST

R.Theiss

Szegedin

Debreczin

Galicia

Cracow

Tarnow

Lemberg

Tarnopol

Stanislaw

R. Dneiper

Carpath

Eperies

Bukovina
occupied
by
Rumania

Botosani

Transylvania

Hermannstadt

Kronstadt

RUMANIA

Bessarabia
(Occupied & claimed by Rumania)

Kishinev

Jassy

Odessa

Galatz

Braila

Dobrudja
claimed
by
Rumania

Bukarest

R. Danube

Orsova

SERBIA

Serajevo

BULGARIA

Rustchuk

Varna

LEGEND

Proposed Internationalised Railways ━━━━━

Internationalised Danube

Line of demarcation between territory
occupied by Czechs and territory not so occupied.
Czech occupation is practically complete N.W. of
this line, except where marked otherwise.

Every square millimeter coloured indicates 225 inhabitants.

Chaque millimètre carré colorié correspond à 225 habitants.

Magyars outside and inside of the proposed boundary line.

Magyars habitant au-de là et au-deçà de la frontière proposée.

Magyars	outside		Magyars	au-de là
	inside			au-de çà

Germans — Allemands
Slovaks — Slovaques
Roumanians — Roumains
Servians — Serbes
Croates — Croates
Ruthenians — Ruthènes
Bunyevatze (Catholic Servians) — Bounievatzes (Serbes catholiques)
Vends (Slovenes) — Vendes (Slovenes)
Bulgarians — Bulgares
Poles — Polonais
Others — Autres
Uninhabited — Pas habité

HELLENISM
IN THE
NEAR EAST

An ethnological map compiled
from the latest statistics by
Professor George Soteriadis
of the University of Athens.

REFERENCE.

- Boundaries of States
- of Northern Epirus
- Florence line (1914)
- Railways

Scale 1: 2,155,000.

English Miles.
10 0 10 20 30 40 50

Kilomètres.
10 5 0 10 20 30 40 50 100

RUMANIA

BUCHAREST

SERBIA

MONTENEGRO

CETINJE

ALBANIA

BULGARIA

SOFIA

Philippopolis

ADRIANOPLE

CONSTANTINOPLE

BLACK SEA

GULF OF MARMARA

SALONICA

Drama

Kavala

Thasos

Samothraki

Imbros

Dedeagatch

Roduto

THESSALY

Corfu

Larissa

Volo

Limnos

Tenedos

Lesbos (Mitylini)

ASIA

SMYRNA

Philadelphia

MINOR

Khios

Preveza

Santa Maura

Cephalonia

Zante

MOREA

ATHENS

Samos

New Ephesus

Andros

Keos

Tinos

Ikaria

Psara

Kythnos

Syra

Mykonos

Patmos

Seriphos

Paros

Naxos

Amorgos

Kos

Siphnos

Siknos

Ios

Astypalea

Nisiros

Milos

Pholegandros

Santorin

Anaphi

RHODOS

Cerigo

Chalki

Karpathos

Kasos

CRETE

IONIAN SEA

ADRIATIC SEA

MEDITERRANEAN SEA

EUBOEA (EGRIPO)

ETHNOLOGICAL STATISTICS OF THRACE & WESTERN ASIA MINOR.

	Bulgarians	Greeks	Mohammedans
A. THRACE.			
(a) Western Thrace (in Bulgarian occupation)	60,878	94,238	284,988
(b) Eastern Thrace (in Turkish occupation)	46,965	272,125	219,323
B. VILAYET OF CONSTANTINOPLE.			
(a) Sandjak of Constantinople	4,331	235,215	306,723
(b) Sandjak of Skutari		74,457	124,281
(c) Sandjak of Chataldja	903	54,787	16,190
C. WESTERN ASIA MINOR			
(a) Independent Government of Ismid		73,134	116,949
(b) Sandjak of Brusa		92,905	215,492
(c) Sandjak of Balikesri		150,946	248,851
(d) Independent Government of Dardanelles		98,836	198,902
(e) Sandjak of Smyrna		449,044	219,494
(f) Sandjak of Magnesia		83,625	247,778
(g) Sandjak of Aidin		54,633	162,554
(h) Sandjak of Mentese		27,708	113,790

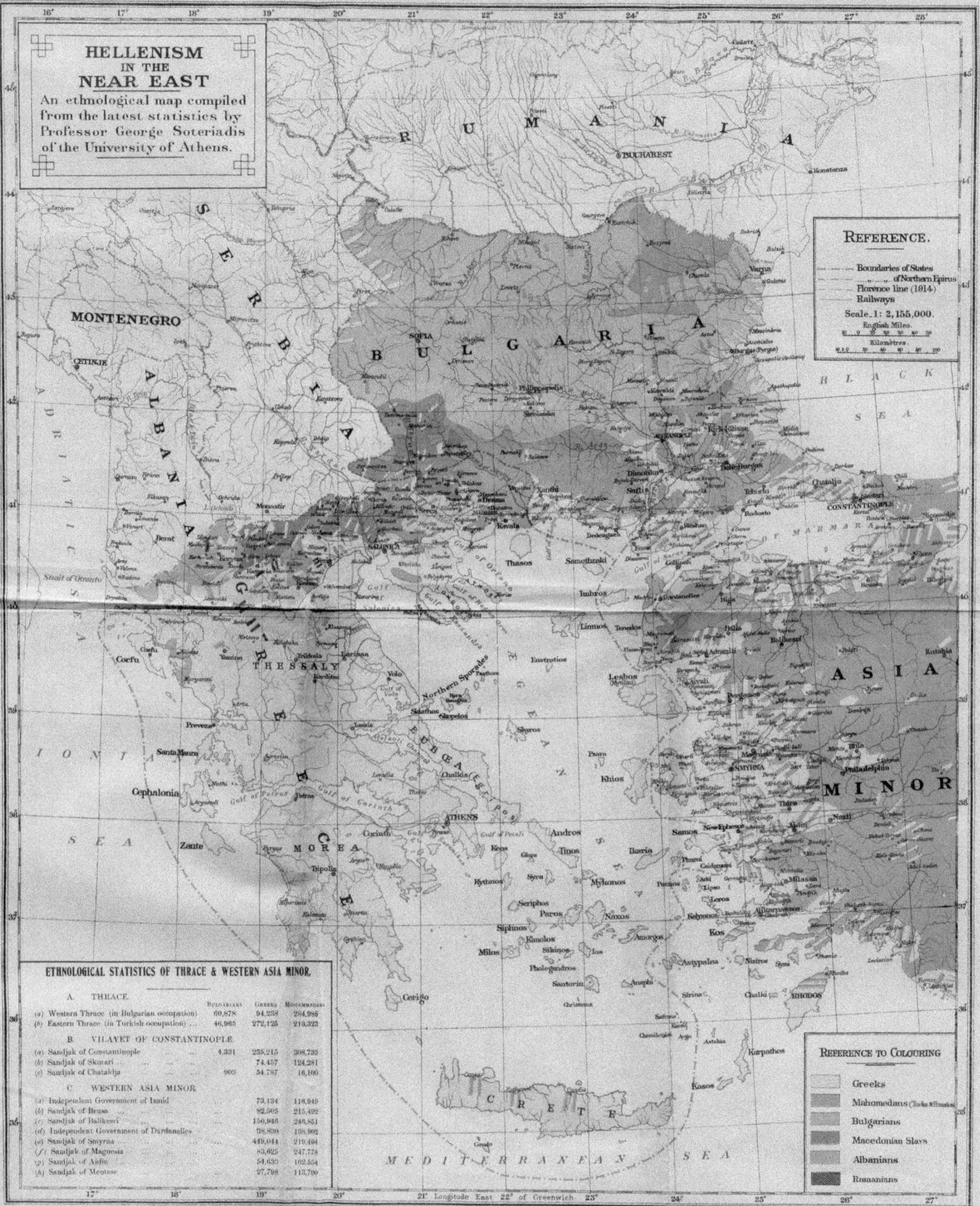

REFERENCE TO COLOURING

- Greeks
- Mahomedans (Turks & Pomaks)
- Bulgarians
- Macedonian Slavs
- Albanians
- Rumanians

Stanford's Geographical Establishment, London.